Birds
& Feathered Friends

TO:

FROM:

Watching birds soar gives me a sense of freedom without limits.

Joy Vizante

The reason birds can fly and we can't is simply because they have perfect faith, for to have faith is to have wings.

J.M. Barrie

The early bird gets the worm, but the second mouse gets the cheese.

Willie Nelson

In order to see birds it is
necessary to become a part
of the silence.

Robert Lynd

Heavenly bodies are nests
of invisible birds.

Dejan Stojanovic

Soft feathers cannot make
a cruel bird kind

Munia Khan

Birds were created to record everything. They were not designed just to be beautiful jewels in the sky, but to serve as the eyes of heaven.

Suzy Kassem

Just as the bird needs wings to fly, a leader needs useful information to flow. Leaders learn.

Israelmore Ayivor

I pray to the birds because they
remind me of what I love rather
than what I fear.

Terry Tempest Williams

This country air, it really is
for them, the birds.

A.D. Aliwat

Birds are magical.
Their flight alone can arouse a
clever thought.

Michael Bassey Johnson

Tweets, real ones, are
meant to signal danger or
find food for baby birds.

A.D. Aliwat

Atop a mountain, one feels as close to the heavens as a bird soaring through the sky.

Jessica Marie Baumgartner

No human ever lived in
a birdless world.

Richard Smyth

Caged birds grow the most colourful wings.

Laura Chouette

The more I work with
birds, the more I believe in
the undreamt, the things
we are not given to know.

Julie Zickefoose

The biggest favor you can do to yourself is fly freely like birds.

Kuldeep Gera

Birds are sky bound;
holding them down in a
cage is wicked love.

Vincent Okay Nwachukwu

The eagle has no fear of adversity. We need to be like the eagle and have a fearless spirit of a conqueror!

Joyce Meyer